EASY JAZZ DUETS FOR 2

TENOR SAXOPHONES

To access audio visit:
www.halleonard.com/mylibrary

8481-7037-2804-0834

ISBN 978-1-59615-608-1

Music Minus One

EXCLUSIVELY DISTRIBUTED BY

Hal•Leonard®

Visit Hal Leonard Online at
www.halleonard.com

Contact Us:
Hal Leonard
7777 West Bluemound Road
Milwaukee, WI 53213
Email: info@halleonard.com

In Europe contact:
Hal Leonard Europe Limited
42 Wigmore Street
Marylebone, London, W1U 2RY
Email: info@halleonardeurope.com

In Australia contact:
Hal Leonard Australia Pty. Ltd.
4 Lentara Court
Cheltenham, Victoria, 3192 Australia
Email: info@halleonard.com.au

The Green Danube

♩ = 152 2 bar drum intro.

Easy

Tone Colors

Reaching Up

♩ = 160 2 bar drum intro.

Easy

Uptown-Downtown

♩ = 126 2 bar drum intro.

6

Main Street

Ski Slope

Easy to Medium

Doin' Your Chores

Easy to Medium

♩ = 138 2 bar bass & drum intro.

Stop and Go

♩ = 132 2 bar bass & drum intro. (pick-up)

Easy to Medium

Glider

Jumper

♩ = 132 2 bar bass & drum intro.

Easy to Medium

Da   Dit

♩ = 126 2 bar drum intro. (pick-up)

Easy to Medium

Hot Fudge

♩ = 132 2 bar bass & drum intro.

Medium

Tijuana

La De Da De

♩ = 108 1½ bar bass & drum intro.

Medium

Switcharoo

♩ = 144 2 bar bass & drum intro.

Medium to Difficult

Swing Easy

♩. = 116 2 bar bass & drum intro.

Medium to Difficult

Hop Scotch

♩ = 120 2 bar bass intro.

Medium to Difficult

Swingin' In The Rain

♩ = 108 2 bar bass & drum intro. (pick-up)

Medium to Difficult

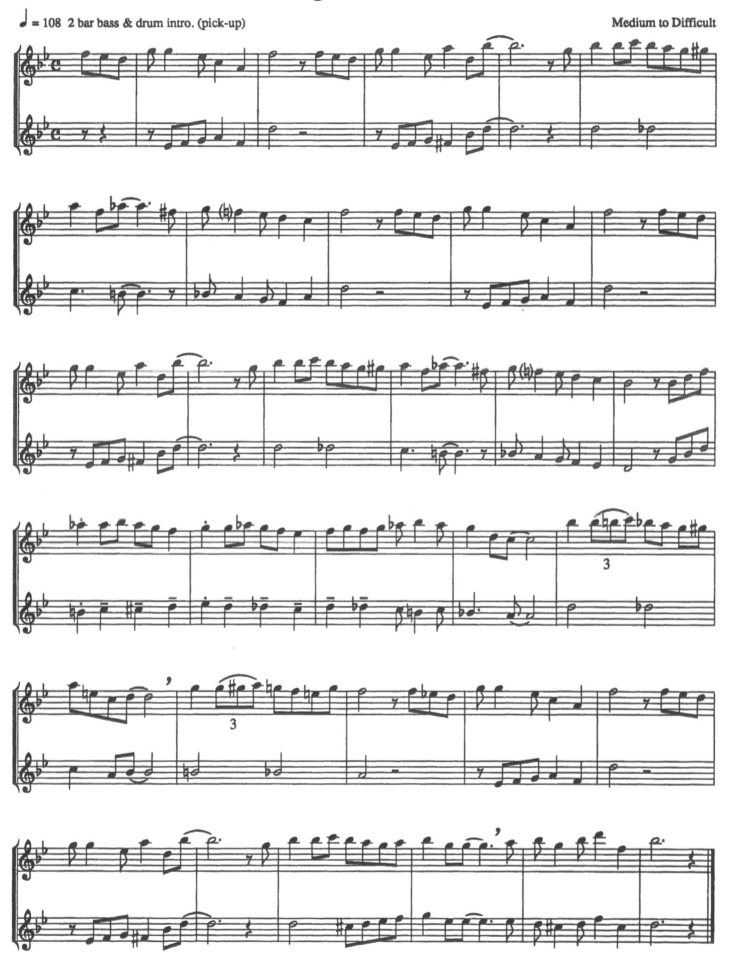

4/4 Waltz

♩ = 168 2 bar drum intro.

Medium to Difficult

One Note Break

Lazy

♩ = 112 2 bar bass intro. (pick-up)

Medium to Difficult

Bits and Pieces

♩ = 152 2 bar drum intro. (pick-up)

Medium to Difficult